Introduc

Hereford is a historic border city surrc
tiful countryside in England, making
All of these fifteen circular self-guided wa
centre, and follow paths and tracks which expiore the little known
Herefordshire countryside with its secret dingles and brooks, its wealth of
broadleaf woods, its cider orchards and its magnificent panoramic views.

A summary of the key characteristics of each walk is given inside the back
cover. This will help you choose, depending upon how much time you have
and how enegetic you feel. A reasonably fit person will be able to tackle any
of them. All the walks follow Public Rights of Way, well established paths
over commons, Forest Enterprise tracks or Permissive Paths. Things can
change however, so do not assume you have gone wrong if what you find
differs from the detail in this book. If you do experience obstructions, these
should be reported to the Herefordshire Rights of Way Officer, telephone
01432 260000, or write to him at PO Box 234, Hereford, HR1 2ZD.

Most walks involve some element of woodland which may have been subsequently harvested and replanted. Similarly young trees grow into mature
ones and may have a major impact on the scenery and/or visibility. In addi-
tion forestry operations may temporarily obstruct or close a section of the
walk. In this situation, please comply with any management notice.

Unless you are negotiating an obstruction you should at all times stay on
the path. Please do not wander onto private land without permission from
the owner. If you are accompanied by a dog, please keep it on a lead at all
times. Many of the walks are well signposted and waymarked, but these posts
and coloured arrows (blue for bridleway, yellow for footpath) are easily van-
dalised and although properly installed may have been removed. Hence the
narrative makes little mention of them.

Apart from walking boots or shoes, which are strongly recommended, no
special equipment is necessary. It is advisable though to carry a waterproof
jacket and some non-alchoholic drink with you at all times of the year. There
are no potentially hazardous situations on any of the walks but it is best to
be prepared for the unexpected and to carry a mobile phone, or a whistle to
attract attention, plus small first aid kit.

The whole area of these walks is in the lee of the Black Mountains and the
weather can be quite localised and subject to sudden change. A weather fore-
cast can be obtained on 09068 400110. Don't forget to leave the location of
your walk with someone and to check-in with them on your return.

Distances from the start of each walk are given in miles radially from
Hereford City centre. The directions, which are from the roundabout junction
of A49, A438 and A465 on the Hereford City inner ring road, give accurate
milages if travelling by road to the start.

Please remember to follow the Country Code and to respect the local tra-
ditions and the environment, so that all those who wish to share the great
charm and beauty of this unspoilt area will remain free to do so.

GARWAY HILL

DESCRIPTION A 3 mile walk over common land with magnificent panoramic viewpoints from which can be seen seven counties. The views extend to the Shropshire hills in the North, the Cotswolds in the East, the North Somerset coast to the South and the Black Mountains of the Brecon Beacons National Park to the West. The walk involves some uphill stretches but they are not severe. There are no stiles and only one gate. Underfoot the paths are firm and grassy. This walk is placed first in this book as it is the author's favourite of all his short circular walks. It can be shortened or extended by taking any of the other paths, tracks and roads shown on the map – all of which are public rights of way.

START From Garway Hill telephone box, 10 miles south west of Hereford. Grid reference SO 448250.

DIRECTIONS Follow the A465 for 8 miles towards Abergavenny, to WORMBRIDGE. Turn LEFT 300 yards after the lay by onto a minor road signed 'GARWAY HILL.' Follow for ³/₄ mile to turn RIGHT at the T-junction. Follow for 1 mile to turn LEFT at the next T-juntion. Continue for a further 1 mile to the hamlet of BAGWYLLYDIART. Ignore the turning to the LEFT and continue for 40 yards to turn RIGHT signed 'GARWAY HILL'. After a ¹/₂ mile at next juntion keep RIGHT and then follow for a further 1 mile – soon with superb views to your LEFT – to park on the grass verge just before the telephone box.

I Walk down the road for 50 yards. Turn RIGHT onto a track with a house on your RIGHT displaying a weathered pub sign of 'The Sun'. This is one of three pubs with related names that used to be in the Garway group of villages. You passed 'The Globe' on your LEFT 100 yards before the start point and 'The Moon' is a mile away on Garway Common. Only the latter is still open. Continue up the track, passing the rebuilt cottage Mount Pleasant on your RIGHT to a gate at the end of the track leading onto

Garway Hill Common. *Before going through the gate lean on the adjacent one on your LEFT to take in the wonderful panorama. From LEFT to RIGHT you will see the Clee Hills, the Malvern Hills, the Cotswolds, May Hill, and the Forest of Dean. Now look to the RIGHT through a gap in the hedge to the beautiful River Monnow valley below you, which separates England and Wales, and beyond over Newport to the North Somerset coast around Clevedon, 35 miles away to the South.*

2 Go through the gate onto the common. Turn RIGHT, and follow a fence line for the first 100 yards, then continue on a wide grassy track towards the top of the hill. *As you ascend you will see ahead of you, to the LEFT of the top of the hill, the Sugar Loaf, a triangular shaped mountain, on the southern end of the Black Mountains. It will disappear as you climb to be replaced by Ysgyryd Fawr, or Holy Mountain, as it gradually comes into view. Its geological slip can be clearly seen, which according to local Welsh folklore is where Noah's Ark finally rested!* Three quarters of the way to the top of the hill you will come to a pond on your RIGHT. It provides water for the ponies that roam the hill. Turn RIGHT here and follow the path to the Radio Mast at the common boundary fence. *To get the best of the panoramic views, move to a small mound 40 yards to the LEFT of the mast to see, from RIGHT to LEFT – Hereford City, the Clee Hills, Wye Valley, Radnor Forest, Hay Bluff, Hatterall Ridge, the entire eastern ridge of the Black Mountains, the Sugar Loaf, Yr Skirrid and Blorenge.*

3 Now with your back to the Radio Mast take the narrow grassy path to the structure on the top of the hill. You are now at 1200 ft. *The building is the remains of an Observation Tower built in World War II but almost immediately redundant due to the arrival of Radar. Alongside it is the Ordnance Survey Tri-angulation Point, once used for map making but now also redundant in an age of aerial photography and satellite surveying. From here you can see seven counties. Can you name them? Answer at bottom of the next page.*

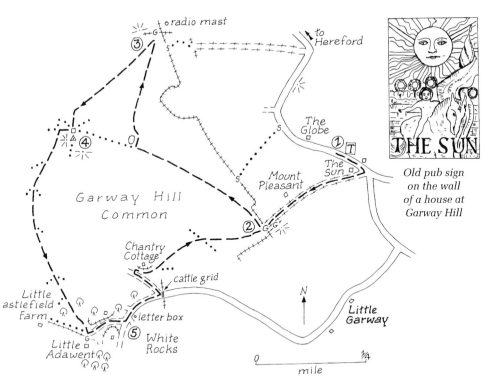

Old pub sign
on the wall
of a house at
Garway Hill

4 Now take the path downhill going West – at right angles to the one you arrived on – after 40 yards you will come to a path intersection. Turn LEFT here *but first pause to look straight ahead below you to Kentchurch Court, the home of the Scudamore family, who still occupy it. A 14thC castle, restored as an Edwardian house by Nash around 1800. Between you and the house is the deer park with it's herd of fallow deer. The house was used by the BBC TV in 2004 for a series about life in an Edwardian country house.* Follow this path, level at first, then downhill to the bottom south east corner of the common. There are a number of tracks crossing your route but the key is to go continuously downhill keeping LEFT and aiming for the nearest corner of a wood with a farm visible beyond it. This should bring you out onto a track at the fenced boundary of the common. Turn LEFT along the track where you should soon pass the gate to Little Adawent cottage on your RIGHT. Now follow the track downhill to join a surfaced road at the hamlet of White Rocks.

5 Turn LEFT along the road passing a converted barn on you RIGHT until you reach a cattle grid. Turn LEFT immediately before it to ascend a track for about 200 yards to the corner of a low stone garden wall on the RIGHT. Turn sharp RIGHT here to follow the garden wall to pass Chantry Cottage. *Built in 1904 and with a plaque in memory of Rev. Jones who provided it, in 1929, as a place of rest and retreat for clergy.* Follow the wall uphill, keeping LEFT where the path forks. The path soon narrows between the bracken. At an intersection of paths keep straight ahead passing under some power lines. Continue uphill to the gate in the RIGHT hand corner of the common. You are now back at point **2**. Retrace your steps to the start point.

From North to West – Herefordshire, Shropshire, Worcestershire, Gloucestershire, Gwent (Monmouthshire), Somerset, Powys (Breckncockshire and Radnorshire)

3

WALK 2

KILPECK AND SADDLEBOW

DESCRIPTION A 6 mile walk, over farmland tracks and paths, through wooded dingles and along ancient hedgerows with constantly changing views of typical Herefordshire mixed farming countryside. The walk involves some gradual ascents and descents as the ground rises from 300 ft at the start to nearly 700 ft at Saddlebow but this ensures some superb views over Hereford City and the Wye Valley. Refreshment is available at the Red Lion pub near the start of the walk. See the map for an optional short cut to make a 3½ mile walk.

START In the car park by the entrance to Kilpeck church 7 miles south west of Hereford. Grid reference SO446305.

DIRECTIONS Follow A465 for 7 miles towards ABERGAVENNY. Turn LEFT signed 'KILPECK'. Continue for half-a-mile to a cross roads. Turn RIGHT and in 300 yards park by the church on your RIGHT.

1 *The walk starts here for an opportunity to visit the church built in 1140 and still retaining much of its Norman character. It has a the unique border of corbel heads depicting both the spiritual and mythalogical, the serious and the amusing, and the pious and the rude. The South door alone justifies a visit with its carved story of Adam and Eve.* With your back to the churchyard gate walk ahead up the street to the Red Lion pub. Turn RIGHT along the road for 150 yards to turn LEFT at the road junction signed VILLAGE HALL. Follow this road for ½ mile, level at first, then rising after passing the village hall to turn RIGHT at a barn onto a track. Go along the track for 50 yards to go through a gate on your LEFT into a meadow. Go diagonally across this field towards some tall scattered trees. *Pause in this field to look RIGHT to Dippersmoor Farm, a fine stone building with a magnificent long barn.* Where the field narrows continue in the same direction to a hedgerow ahead, keeping a few scattered mature oaks to your RIGHT. Ignore the

fence and stile above you on your LEFT. On reaching the hedge turn RIGHT along it to cross a gate with stile where it meets a wood. Now follow the edge of the wood. *There are fine views along here.* Where it ends turn LEFT along the hedgerow for 50 yards to turn RIGHT through a gate into a meadow. Go diagonally downhill, with a wood on your LEFT, to cross a gate with stile.

2 Turn LEFT along the track in front of the cottages. After a 100 yards enter the corner of a wood over a stile. Follow the winding path through the wood to another stile then over a ditch to turn LEFT to a further stile into a meadow. Follow the hedge on your LEFT with a new dormer house on your RIGHT to the end of the field to cross a stile in the hedge ahead of you 10 yards from the corner of the field. Now turn LEFT to go uphill on the LEFT of two tracks. *As you ascend there some fine views particularly of Garway Hill* (**Walk 1**) *with its distinctive radio mast.* Just before the top of the hill the track divides, turn LEFT through a gate onto a grassy track with a house – Grafton Oak – on your LEFT. Go through another gate into a meadow with a fence on your RIGHT. Follow the fence until you come to a stile on your RIGHT. Do not cross the stile. Along this fence line there are fine views of Saddlebow Hill – the object of your walk. Saddlebow is the wooded hill on the RIGHT with Cole's Tump on the LEFT. *Tump is a local word meaning anything from a burial mound to a significant hill.*

3 Now bear away from the fence to go diagonally down hill towards the tree lined brook. 30 yards up from the bottom corner of the field cross a stile into the next field. Ignore the footbridge below you. Follow the brook and hedge on your LEFT through the next two fields. After 120 yards in the third field cross the stream by the footbridge. Now go diagonally uphill to cross a stile with a gate in the hedge on your RIGHT. Follow the fence on your RIGHT for 200 yards to cross a stile opposite Greenways farm. Keep close to the fence on your LEFT, go through the copse ahead to emerge, via a stile, back into the field. Go straight ahead uphill to a gate in the top RIGHT hand corner of the field. *Turn around here to enjoy the panorama of the Black Mountains to the West, the Wye Valley ahead and the Malverns to the East.* Ignore the track to your RIGHT, cross the stile to continue uphill diagonally across the field to a gate by an ancient oak. Cross the next field to a gate in the top LEFT corner. Continue with the hedge on your LEFT to a gate onto a minor road.

4 Turn LEFT onto the road to go gently uphill. *Where there are gaps in the hedge, pause to take in the magnificent views.* After 700 yards, where the hedge and the line of the telegraph poles bears away from the road on the LEFT, take the sign posted narrow path downhill through the bracken. The path widens between trees to join a track. Turn RIGHT for a few yards then turn LEFT on joining a metalled road leading to a farm. Turn RIGHT immediately before the first building to go down an old green lane. Continue to the end to cross a gate into a meadow. Follow the hedge on your RIGHT to a gate just beyond an ancient oak. Turn RIGHT here onto a farm track and follow it, first with the hedge on your RIGHT then it changes to the LEFT until it reaches a track inter-section at the end of the field. Turn LEFT here through the second gate on your LEFT and follow the hedge to the farm buildings ahead. Go through the gate with stile onto the surfaced road through the farmyard.

5 Continue along this minor road. After 500 yards at the road juntion keep RIGHT and continue for a further 150 yards to pass a house and barns on your LEFT. Turn LEFT here between the last of the barns and some derelict ground to go downhill across a field, keeping parallel to the hedge on your LEFT. At the line of trees at the bottom of the field turn RIGHT and follow the hedge to a gap in it about 10 yards before the hedge changes direction. Cross the stile to go through two fields making for a farmhouse ahead on your RIGHT. Cross a stile onto a private drive between the house and the

barns. Continue to the end of the drive to turn LEFT and almost immediately RIGHT at the Red Lion pub back to the start.

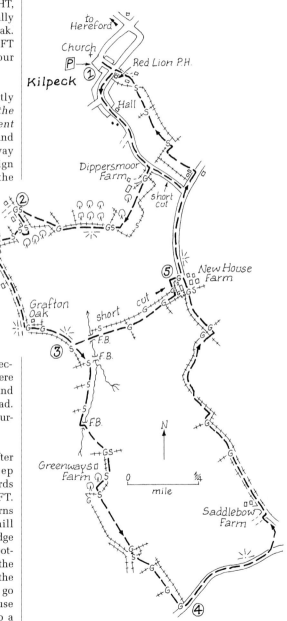

5

THE MARCLE RIDGE

DESCRIPTION A 4 mile walk over farm and woodland paths and tracks, of which 1½ miles is along the Marcle Ridge with its spectacular panoramas. The Ridge is an ancient route evidenced by the numerous Iron Age and Roman settlements along either side. The walk starts at 635ft and rises to 758ft at the highest point. It then descends to the western valley and then after 1 mile along the valley floor ascends back up to the Ridge. The steepest gradient is 1 in 10 and the effort of this moderate climb is well worth it for the outstanding views. The west of the Ridge is mainly wooded, so in summer the views are to the east but as the trees are deciduous the winter months provide views in all directions. See the map for an optional short cut to make a 3 mile walk.

START The Marcle Ridge car park and picnic site, 8½ miles south east of Hereford. Grid reference SO 630346.

DIRECTIONS Take the A438 signed for LEDBURY. On the outskirts of the city centre and 200 yards passed the Fire Station turn RIGHT signed 'FOWNHOPE B4224'. After 3½ miles in MORDIFORD keep straight ahead to the Moon Inn, then keep LEFT signed 'WOOLHOPE 3'. In WOOLHOPE turn LEFT passed the Crown Inn and take the second LEFT signed 'LEDBURY'. Keep RIGHT through the next village and at the junction turn RIGHT signed 'MUCH MARCLE 4'. Go up the hill and along the ridge for 1½ miles to the picnic site at the next junction.

From the car park go up the steps in the fork of the Y-junction into a field. Follow the edge of the field with woods on your RIGHT for the whole length of the ridge. (There is a parallel path which enters the wood shortly after the the end of the second field but this is not advised as it can be overgrown and obstruct your views). *At the end of the second field stop to enjoy the panorama. If you take the hedgerow as 12 o'clock, then the Malvern Hills stretch on the*

horizon from 10 to 12, Ledbury in the middle distance is at 11, Bredon Hill at 12, the Cotswolds from 12 to 2, May Hill at 2 and the TV mast at 2.30. The village of Much Marcle is below you at 1.30 with its distinctive Old Red Sandstone tower. Much Marcle is home to Westons cider and perry and offers tours of the mill. It has a museum, shop, cafe, and wildlife park. Continue along the ridge and you will soon reach the field with the mast. *This is a major TV and Radio transmitter for the area. Note the massive anchorages for the supporting guys and how they are irregularly placed to compensate for the prevailing wind.* After leaving this field stop at the next stile with May Hill ahead on the skyline. *This hill with its distinctive clump of trees is owned by the National Trust and although not particularly high at 971ft is a major landmark and can be seen from as far away as the Somerset coast. Younger trees have been planted around the mature ones so that this crown of trees should always be visible.* The next stile is your last along the ridge.

2 Cross the stile and turn RIGHT onto a track going downhill. *Look LEFT for fine views of typical Herefordshire farms with their cider orchards adjacent to the farmhouse.* As you descend Oldbury Camp Iron Age fort comes into view, the outline of the protective earthworks can still be seen. Ignore all paths off this track until it levels out, then turn off to the RIGHT over a stile into a field (if you reach a barn you have come 10 yards too far). Keep the fence on your LEFT to cross another stile 50 yards ahead. Then turn RIGHT onto a farm track and follow through two fields, keeping the hedge on your RIGHT, to cross a ford (negotiable on foot in all but extreme flood conditions). Now stay on the track going uphill to join the minor road from the picnic site. Turn LEFT onto the road and go downhill to a road junction. Turn RIGHT a few yards before it through double gates onto a tree lined track. Follow this level track with a fence on your LEFT towards farm buildings. As you approach the farmyard keep to the field, passing a pond on your RIGHT to a gate into the farmyard.

3 Go through the gate and follow the farm track to the LEFT, after a few yards at the end of an open barn with farm buildings behind it, turn sharp RIGHT up a track into the wood. Follow the track to the edge of the wood to a stile into an arable field. There is no clearly defined path across it but it should follow the course shown on the sketch map to a gate in the far top LEFT corner of the field into the wood Alternatively for a longer but easier route follow the wide grass verge around the edge of the wood. Go through the wood to a gate at the far end into a meadow. Cross the meadow keeping parallel to the wood on your RIGHT to a mound ahead. *Pause to take in the panorama to your LEFT of the Black Mountains with Hay Bluff on the northern end. The village of Woolhope is below you. The foreground is part of the Woolhope Dome – an area of limestone surrounded by the more typical red soil of Herefordshire and its underlying Old Red Sandstone. It explains the mound ahead which will turn out to be lime kilns.* At them turn RIGHT and make for a gate and stile at the end of the wood.

4 Go downhill along the edge of the wood. Leave the wood through a gate or stile to go downhill at first to the floor of the valley then ascend to the ridge keeping the hedge to your LEFT. Just before the ridge go through a gate into a short length of green lane to join a minor road. You are now at Hooper`s Oak. *In 1575, about half-a-mile from here, a landslip buried buildings. A house near the site is called The Wonder in memory of this catastrophic event.* Turn RIGHT here and follow the road for half-a-mile back to the picnic site.

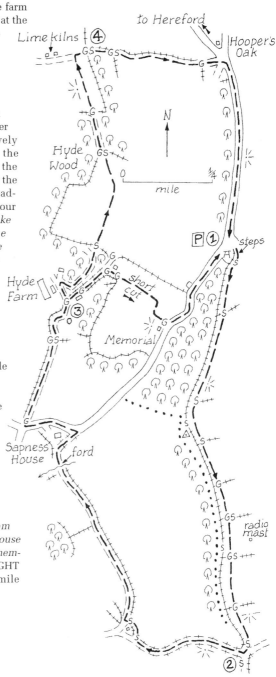

7

ATHELSTAN'S WOOD

DESCRIPTION A 5 mile undulating farmland and woodland walk which can be shortened to 2½ miles. Athelstan's Wood is an ancient wood named after a Bishop of Hereford in 1056. The route provides superb panoramic views over the south Herefordshire countryside, to the Malvern Hills in the east, the Forest of Dean in the south and the Welsh Black Mountains to the west

START From St David's church, Little Dewchurch, 5½ miles south east of Hereford. Grid reference SO 529317

DIRECTIONS Take the A49 going south, after ½ mile turn LEFT at traffic lights signed 'HOLME LACY' and after a further 300 yards turn RIGHT at roundabout signed 'LITTLE DEWCHURCH 5'. In LITTLE DEWCHURCH turn RIGHT signed 'ST. DAVIDS CHURCH'. Continue for ½ mile to park in the lay-by at the church.

Note: Altwyn Farm is a diary farm and if the weather is wet, or during the winter months, the farm-yard can be very muddy and/or covered in slurry. In these conditions it may be best to follow the road from the church to the farm. Even along this lane there are lovely views ahead towards Ross-on-Wye.

I St. David's church dates from the 14thC but only traces are now left of the original. It was rebuilt in 1869. With your back to the church take the lane to your RIGHT. After 30 yards turn LEFT and follow the lane gently uphill for ½ mile where a short grassy track turns sharp LEFT to cross a stile and gate into a field. Continue 40 yards downhill to go through a double gate and stile on your RIGHT into a field. Then follow a delightful stream on your LEFT downhill through two fields. In the second field you will pass a footbridge and shortly after join a track which crosses the stream. Do not cross the stream but turn RIGHT to follow the waymarked track uphill, with a hedge on your RIGHT, to join a short green lane into

the farmyard. Go straight ahead through the yard, with one or more gates, to rejoin the lane from the church.

2 Go straight ahead down the lane to the bottom of the hill and turn RIGHT onto a track with a gate and stile 40 yards ahead. The 2½ mile walk leaves this route here.

3 Cross the stile and continue for 30 yards. Now turn LEFT uphill on a footpath at the edge of the wood to a pedestrian gate into a field. Go straight ahead and to the LEFT of three oak trees. A hedge will soon come into sight, keep it on your LEFT and follow it to a gate and stile in the corner of the field.

4 Cross the stile to turn RIGHT onto a waymarked track, which becomes a green lane, and follow it for ½ mile, ignoring all other paths or tracks to right and left. On reaching the first building on your RIGHT – Lower House Farm – from here the track is metalled. Continue to St Mary's church. Little Birch is on your LEFT.

5 Immediately after the church turn RIGHT down a track to reach Higgin's Well at the bottom. *The well was restored for Queen Victoria's Diamond Jubilee in 1897. Legend has it that the landowner tried to stop local people drawing water from it but after his own house was flooded he relented and the well has never run dry since!* Now turn LEFT to take the uphill track behind the well. A short stretch of this can be muddy, though some stepping stones are provided. At the next track junction turn RIGHT and continue uphill to meet the metalled road.

6 Turn RIGHT and follow the road uphill to where it ends at a track with a finger post. Turn RIGHT here. After passing a house – Bwthyn Tir Glas/Green Lea Cottage – continue straight ahead to a gate into a green lane. Follow this track gently downhill, going through one more gate, to the end where it crosses a farm track connecting two fields. Enter the wood ahead and follow the path until it meets a wider forest track. *You are now back in Athelstan's Wood with its magnificent Redwoods, Douglas Fir, Western*

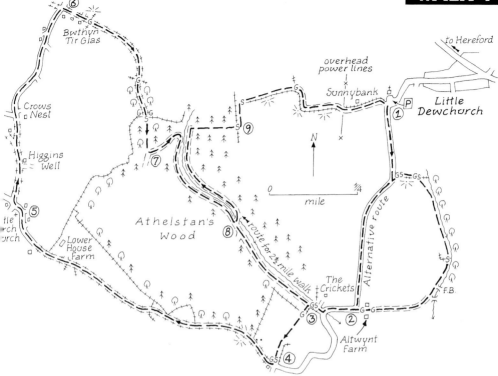

Hemlock, blue bells in spring and maybe, if you are quiet, a chance to see Fallow Deer.

7 Turn LEFT here and follow the track downhill where the track swings to the RIGHT and runs parrallel with a stream on your LEFT. Continue downhill for about ¹/₂ mile to a track junction where a track to the LEFT crosses the stream by a culvert.

8 Cross the stream and turn sharp LEFT to follow the track uphill, with the stream now below you on your LEFT, for about ¹/₂ mile to the end of the track. Go to the far end of the clearing then turn RIGHT up an embankment onto a waymarked footpath between the trees. Follow to cross a stile at the edge of the wood.

9 Turn LEFT here to follow the field edge uphill to cross another stile into a meadow. Turn RIGHT to follow the fence on your RIGHT to a gate. *There are magnificent views along this section of the walk from the*

Malvern Hills in the East, then clockwise May Hill, Penyard Hill, Ross-on-Wye, the Forest of Dean, the top of the Sugar Loaf and, to the far West, the Hatterall Ridge on the Welsh Black Mountains. Can you identify May Hill, a significant landmark in Gloucestershire with its clump of trees on the summit of this rounded hill? Or how about finding the stately church spire at Ross-on-Wye? Go through the gate and follow the track, level at first then, once under the pyloned power lines, downhill to rejoin the road, turning LEFT for the church car park back at the start.

THE 2¹/₂ MILE WALK

Follow the main walk to point **3**, then cross the stile and continue straight ahead up the forest track for about ¹/₂ mile with the stream and some ponds on your RIGHT until you reach a track juntion where a track crosses the stream by a culvert. You have now rejoined the main walk at point **8**.

9

WALK 5

VOWCHURCH COMMON

DESCRIPTION A varied 6 mile walk over farm and woodland tracks with delightful views and constantly changing scenery. The walk rises from 360ft at the start to 785ft but the ascent is broken by some short level sections and a 1 mile gently rising ridge walk.

START Lay-by opposite Vowchurch church, 10 miles south west of Hereford. Grid reference SO 362365

DIRECTIONS Take A465 toward ABERGAVENNY. 2 miles from HEREFORD turn RIGHT onto B4349 signed 'HAY ON WYE'. After 2 miles, in CLEHONGER, turn LEFT signed 'HAY ON WYE'. After joining B4348 continue for a further 3 miles and in a hidden dip, turn LEFT signed 'VOWCHURCH' and after 200 yards park opposite the church.

1 Walk back to cross the main road (with extreme caution in the hidden dip). Go uphill on a minor road signed VOWCHURCH COMMON (PRIVATE LAND). Turn off the road onto a track immediately before the first house on the LEFT. Follow it for about ½ mile as it changes to a green lane and then to a footpath until you reach a waymarked path on the LEFT. Continue for 10 yards to turn RIGHT up a steep footpath between gardens, then crossing a track and finally over a stile into a wood before joining the road again. Turn LEFT and go uphill for about 200 yards to the first house, Juniper Cottage, on the RIGHT.

2 Turn RIGHT immediately after it to go along a footpath to a stile onto Vowchurch Common. *Stop here to enjoy the spectacular panorama. From LEFT to RIGHT – The Malvern Hills, May Hill, Orcop Hill, Saddlebow* (**Walk 2**)*, Garway Hill* (**Walk 1**)*, The Graig, Ysgyryd (probably the best vantage point to view the slip on that hill), and the Black Mountains. The landowner has thoughtfully provided seats to view in comfort but please keep to the footpath as this is*

private land. Turn LEFT along the top of the Common and follow the footpath through scrub. After some stiles, a gate and some steps, enter a meadow by a gate. A few yards into the field a house will be seen on the LEFT, go through the gate into the garden to pass between the house and a barn. Exit by a gate to cross an access track to a stile into a meadow. Beware of the long drop on the far side. Go downhill with the hedge on your RIGHT to a stile in front of a white cottage.

3 Turn LEFT onto a lane and go downhill to a gate into a meadow with a derelict building on your LEFT. Continue downhill with the hedge on your RIGHT until the field becomes a wide track, then after 50 yards turn LEFT over a ditch through a gate on your LEFT into a meadow. Now follow the hedge on your LEFT. As you near the end of the field cross a footbridge 50 yards to the LEFT of a half-timbered farmhouse. Turn LEFT along the track leading to Monnington Court farm buildings. *Look LEFT to a clump of trees, they hide a Motte and Bailey. Adjacent are ancient barns but the red brick farmhouse is Georgian.* Go through a gate to continue on the track for 100 yards, turn LEFT off it here over a stile into a field.

4 Go uphill to enter the wood ahead by a gate. Keep on the main track generally going uphill until you reach the wider metalled forest track along the ridge. Turn LEFT along it until you come to the first main intersection. Turn RIGHT then immediately LEFT and follow the grass track, gently ascending, to a gate into a field. Now follow the edge of the wood for ½ mile. *There are continous panoramic views along this ridge from the Malvern Hills in the east, Wye Valley below you and the Radnor Hills to the west. Near the end of this section a large farmhouse will come into view – Sheep Pasture Farm – a prosiac name for such a grand building.* 100yds before the house turn into the wood through a gate and walk along the edge of it to emerge onto the drive to the house. Go straight ahead and follow the drive for nearly ½ mile to where it turns sharp RIGHT.

10

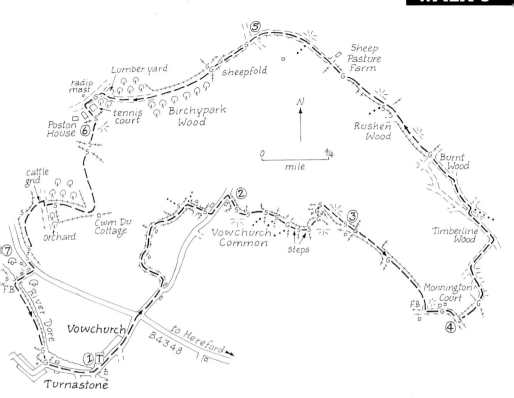

5 Turn off the main track here, ignore the gate on your LEFT to Hill Farm, go straight ahead down a lane between hedges to a gate and continue until reaching a sheepfold. Go through the gate on the LEFT into the wood. Keep to the RIGHT in the wood. *You are now at the highest point of you walk at 785ft.* Continue until you reach a lumber area, then turn LEFT at a track junction and go towards buildings – Poston Lodge Farm. Immediately after a tennis court on your LEFT turn LEFT, with the farm buildings on your RIGHT, to a stile into a meadow. *Pause here for the view and to look back to Poston House – an exceptionally fine building.*

6 Cross the narrowest part of the meadow keeping just to the LEFT of the start of a valley – Cwm Du – to cross a stile by some mature oaks into a patch of scrub. Go steeply down through it for a few yards to cross a stile into another meadow. Go down the valley to buildings – Cwm Cottage – with a

view of the village of Vowchurch beyond it. From the cottage go diagonally uphill to the top LEFT corner of the wood. Cross a stile into an orchard, keeping to the top boundary. When you reach the road turn RIGHT over a cattle grid and then immediately LEFT to go downhill across the narrowest part of the meadow to join a hedgerow on your RIGHT. Follow this, ignoring the first stile, to cross the next one into a belt of trees. Go downhill for a few yards to a stile onto the main road.

7 Cross this busy road with caution and turn LEFT. After 50 yards turn into the Caravan Park, go straight ahead, passing Reception to cross the River Dore by a footbridge. Turn LEFT and follow the river until you reach a gate, then cross a small field to a gate to the LEFT of Turnastone Church onto the road. Turn LEFT and follow the road back to the start. *You will pass Turnastone Court, an interesting building owned by the Countryside Restoration Trust.*

BRIDGE SOLLERS & PRESTON ON WYE

DESCRIPTION An easy 6 mile almost level walk over farmland, through orchards, a vineyard and finally along the river Wye giving some fine views of the Wye Valley countryside. The route crosses some arable fields which after heavy rain could be muddy. It can be shortened to 3 miles. Refreshment is available at the Yew Tree pub in Preston on Wye half-way through the walk.

START Bridge Sollers 5 miles west of Hereford. Grid reference SO 411424.

DIRECTIONS Take the A438 towards BRECON, and after 6 miles turn LEFT onto a minor road signed 'MADLEY & PRESTON ON WYE'. Cross over the River Wye and after 200 yards park on the LEFT under some walnut trees just passed a half-timbered house.

I Walk a few yards further on from the parking place to turn RIGHT off the road onto a track. Follow the track through three fields to where the hedge ends on your RIGHT. Now go straight ahead across an arable field keeping parallel with the hedge on your LEFT to cross a footbridge in a gap in the line of trees ahead. The short walk leaves the main walk here.

2 To continue the main walk turn RIGHT and follow the hedgerow around the field to a gate into a meadow. Go diagonally across the field to a gate in the far LEFT corner. Now follow the hedge on your RIGHT for 1/2 mile. *You are on the top of an embankment which was probably an ancient course of the River Wye. There are fine views across the valley to Garnons Hill with Offa,s Dyke running along its ridge, but hidden now by the trees, and also of the grand house of Garnons.* Near the end of the meadow, where a track bears away from the hedge, keep close to the hedge and go to the top corner to go over a double stile into a cider orchard.

3 Turn RIGHT and follow the hedge on your RIGHT around the edge of the orchard until you reach a gate into a lane. Turn LEFT but then keep RIGHT, ignoring a track immediately to your LEFT, and follow the lane to the first house, where it becomes a surfaced road, and continue into the village. *Preston on Wye is quietly attractive with its wide street and three well manicured village greens with a walnut tree on the first one you come to. You will pass two chapels – Baptist and Primitive Methodist – but the Parish church stands by itself nearer the river. There was a ferry between the village and Bycross until the early 1900s and a ford 1 mile downstream at Byford but there was no bridge until Bridge Sollers was built in 1896 and replaced by the present one in 2004.* Continue through the village passing the Yew Tree pub on your RIGHT and keeping LEFT at the first road junction. Then after a 1/2 mile when the road bears LEFT go straight ahead along a track with a derelict building between road and track.

4 Go along this track, which soon narrows to footpath width, with a number of easy to open bridleway gates. When the track ends at the third gate into an arable field go diagonally across it to a waymarked post in the hedge on the RIGHT about a 100 yards before the next gate. Continue with the hedge on you RIGHT along a field boundary to cross two more arable fields to a gate leading to a green lane. Continue along the lane to pass between a house and a small pond onto a road. Turn LEFT onto the road and go down it (with extreme caution as it is narrow and busy) until you reach the end of the hop fields on your RIGHT. Continue for a few yards to a gap in the hedge.

5 Go through the gap into a vineyard. Keep to the hedge on your RIGHT to go through another gap in the hedge straight ahead. Turn RIGHT and follow

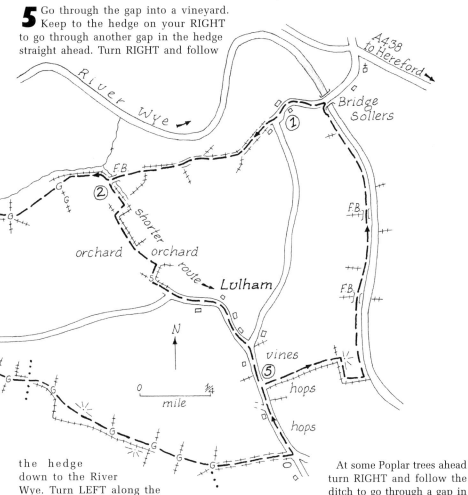

the hedge down to the River Wye. Turn LEFT along the bank and follow for 1/2 mile back to Bridge Sollers. *Keep an eye open for Cormorants, they are often seen on the high dead branches of oak trees on the far bank drying their outstretched wings. You will notice the attractive but invasive pink flowers on long fleshy stems along the river bank. This is Himalayan Balsam, it is not a native of this country and in view of its rampant and widespread growth, there is considerable conservation effort to get rid of it.*

THE 3 MILE WALK

Follow the main walk to point **2**, then turn LEFT and follow the hedge on your LEFT.

At some Poplar trees ahead turn RIGHT and follow the ditch to go through a gap in the hedge ahead into a cider orchard. Turn LEFT and follow the hedge on your LEFT until it turns LEFT then go straight ahead through the middle of the orchard to a hedge. Turn RIGHT here to go up a short hill to a stile in the corner of the orchard into a field. Follow the hedge on your LEFT to a minor road. Turn LEFT and follow it to a road junction. Turn RIGHT and go up the road (with care as you are now on a much busier road) for about 300 yards to a gap in the hedge on your LEFT (if you reach a hop field you have come a few yards too far). You have now reached point **5** on the main walk.

BODENHAM & THE RIVER LUGG

DESCRIPTION An easy 5 mile walk along the River Lugg, through farmland, woods and lanes It is typical of the Lugg Valley countryside. There is an opportunity to visit the the nearby Bodenham Lakes – a 110 acre nature reserve managed by the Herefordshire Parks and Countryside Service. The lakes are a prime site in Herefordshire for bird watching, especially for migrant waterfowl and there is a bird hide for viewing. The reserve also has two orchards with 38 different types of dessert and culinary apples in one and 11 different perry and 19 cider apples in the other. A visit to the reserve at the beginning or end of your walk will add a further 1½ miles – just follow the map. See the map for an optional short cut to make a 2½ mile walk.

START From the car park in Bodenham, 7 miles north of Hereford. Grid reference SO 530510.

DIRECTIONS Take A49 towards LEOMINSTER for 6½ miles. Shortly after starting to go uphill through the woods, filter and turn RIGHT signed 'BODENHAM 2'. Continue for 1½ miles to turn RIGHT into the village to park opposite the school.

I From the car park walk towards the church. Go through the Lych Gate into the churchyard and follow the path keeping RIGHT around the church to a gate in the far corner. *The church is 14thC and is worth a visit. Externally the tower looks strange with its truncated spire but the money ran out at the rebuild in 1889!* Cross a ditch by a footbridge, there is now a gate and turnstile on the RIGHT into the nature reserve. To continue the walk ignore them and cross the main footbridge over the River Lugg. *The word 'Lugg' seems an ugly name for such a beautiful river but its Celtic meaning of 'bright water' is far more descriptive.* Now turn RIGHT and follow the river bank

to the end of the field. Cross a double stile and footbridge then turn RIGHT into the next field. After 30 yards leave the hedge and take a footpath across the field to an embankment on the far side. Cross another footbridge and stiles, then up a short slope into another field. Again cross this field to a gap in the hedge on the far side. Continue over a stile onto a drive to the house on your RIGHT. Go straight ahead to join a public road. *You are now at The Vern – once an ancient settlement with a ford over the river.* Turn LEFT onto the road and continue for ½ mile to a road T-junction. *Bannut Tree House on the corner was once an inn – a bannut is a walnut.*

2 Turn LEFT at the T-junction and go along the road for 150 yds to cross a stile on your RIGHT. Go through four meadows to a footbridge into a short section of green lane. Cross the stile at the end onto a track with a house on your RIGHT. After a few yards there is a 'No Right Of Way' sign. Turn sharp RIGHT immediately before it onto a garden path leading to private property – Monmarsh End. On reaching the house turn LEFT to pass the front door to a stile into a meadow. *This route seems somewhat intrusive but it is the authorised Right Of Way and the owners do display a notice on the stile 'Trespassers Will Be Welcome'. However in spite of their welcome, please do respect their privacy.* Continue across three meadows. In the third, aim to the LEFT of a solitary oak tree and about 150 yards to the RIGHT of a gate in the LEFT corner of the field. This brings you to some planks over a ditch and after a further 20 yards to a gate in the hedge onto a road.

3 Turn RIGHT onto the road, then after 20 yards turn LEFT over a stile into a meadow. Go uphill to a stile in the top RIGHT corner, then to another in the far LEFT corner of the next field. Go straight ahead to another stile onto a green lane. Turn LEFT here and follow it for ½ mile when a house roof should be visible on your LEFT. Turn LEFT here over a stile to follow, initially with a hedge and house on your RIGHT, through two meadows. At the end of the second cross a stile and turn RIGHT into a lane leading to

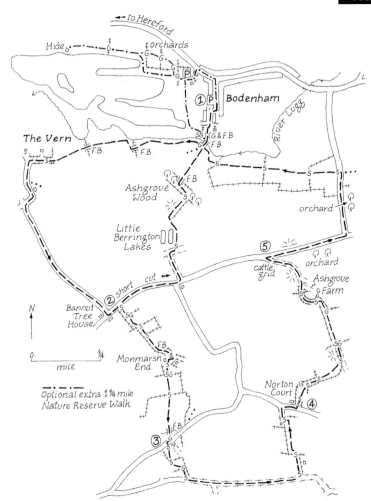

a road. Turn RIGHT onto the road to a wall around Norton Court on your LEFT.

4 Turn LEFT at the end of the wall over a stile into a meadow. Go uphill to the top RIGHT corner to a stile onto a short fenced path to another stile into the next meadow. *From here there are surprisingly magnificent views as you are only at 345 ft and yet there is a panorama from The Marcle Ridge* (**Walk 3**) *to Hay Bluff in the Black Mountains some 21 miles away.* Now bear half-LEFT to a stile in the hedge ahead onto a wide grassy track. Turn LEFT and follow it to Ash Grove Farm ahead. Just before reaching a gate across the track into the farm turn LEFT over a stile signed 'Permissive Path' and follow it on a semi-circular route between willow hedges around the house to join the drive. Turn LEFT along it to a cattle grid where it joins a minor road.

5 Turn RIGHT along the road and follow it for 550 yards to turn LEFT at the first road junction. Then after a further 400 yards turn LEFT over a stile into a meadow. Cross two more meadows with stiles to bring you back to the River Lugg where you cross the footbridge to retrace your steps back to the start.

WALK 8

STOKE LACY & ULLINGSWICK

DESCRIPTION A 5 mile walk over farmland, through woods and along the alder tree lined banks of the River Loddon. There are some gentle rolling hills but it is an easy walk and refreshment is available at two inns along the walk. The route passes through the delightful and tranquil village of Ullingswick

START From the car park opposite Stoke Lacy church 9 miles north east of Hereford. Grid reference SO 621494.

DIRECTIONS Take A465 towards WORCESTER. After 2½ miles turn LEFT off the WORCESTER road to continue on the A465 towards BROMYARD. Then after a further 7½ miles at the bottom of the hill in STOKE LACY turn RIGHT signed 'HOPTON 1' and park on the RIGHT opposite the church.

I *Stoke Lacy nestles around the River Loddon. The Rectory, opposite the church, was the birthplace of the founder of Morgan Cars which are still built in Malvern only a few miles away. There is a memorial stained glass window in the church porch depicting two of the famous three wheeled vehicles. The village was also famous for its Symonds Cider which was made here from 1727 until recently when the replacement modern buildings were taken over by a local brewery. The church has Norman origins but was rebuilt in 1863.* To start the walk go back to cross over the main road. Turn LEFT for 40 yards then RIGHT onto an access track between houses and follow it until it ends at a double garage to the LEFT of a house. Go through a gate to the LEFT of the garage into a field. Cross the field to a stile and footbridge into a large meadow. Bear LEFT across it towards a line of trees which hide the River Loddon. Follow the river along until the remains of a red brick building – Huddle Mill – can be seen behind the hedge.

2 Turn LEFT across a footbridge into the bottom of a field and then straight ahead

to cross another footbridge opposite it over the River Loddon. Turn RIGHT and follow the river through three fields. At the end of the third, where the river bears away to the RIGHT, go straight ahead with a fence and house on your RIGHT. After passing the house turn RIGHT through a gate into a small paddock to another gate onto a drive to the house. Turn LEFT down the drive to join a minor road. Turn RIGHT for 5 yards then LEFT up some steps then 20 yards to a stile into a short green lane (overgrown in 2004 and, if still so, walk to the RIGHT of it) leading to a stile into a meadow. Continue ahead to pass between a copse on your LEFT and a hedge on your RIGHT into a cider orchard until you come to a gate. Go through to pass to the RIGHT of a cottage and then through double gates to turn RIGHT onto a minor road

3 Follow the road until you reach the Three Horseshoes Inn on your LEFT. Turn LEFT immediately after it up a track until you come to a complex track junction. Ignore all gates, tracks to houses and and into a wood, to continue straight ahead on the only track which goes downhill to a gate into a meadow with a wood on your RIGHT. *For the next ½ mile there are superb views, from the Marcle Ridge Mast in the south east (Walk 3), May Hill, Garway Hill Mast (Walk 1), Ysgyryd Fawr, The Sugar Loaf and The Black Mountains in the West some 24 miles away.* After two more gates enter Boxash Wood and follow the edge of the wood into a meadow. Then follow the hedge on your LEFT through two more gates to a track junction. Ignore the track to your LEFT and go straight ahead through a gate then along a hedge to another gate on your LEFT at the end of a field.

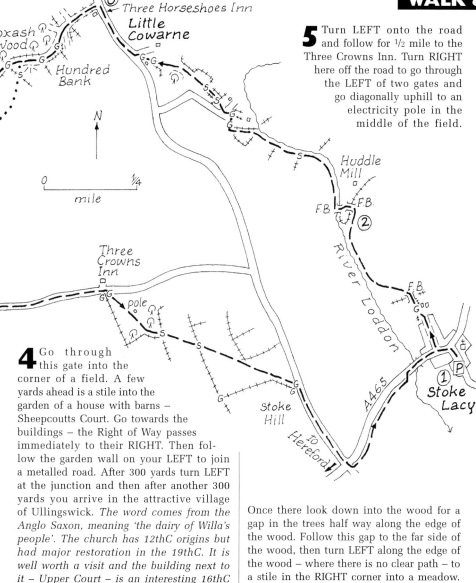

5 Turn LEFT onto the road and follow for ¹/₂ mile to the Three Crowns Inn. Turn RIGHT here off the road to go through the LEFT of two gates and go diagonally uphill to an electricity pole in the middle of the field.

4 Go through this gate into the corner of a field. A few yards ahead is a stile into the garden of a house with barns – Sheepcoutts Court. Go towards the buildings – the Right of Way passes immediately to their RIGHT. Then follow the garden wall on your LEFT to join a metalled road. After 300 yards turn LEFT at the junction and then after another 300 yards you arrive in the attractive village of Ullingswick. *The word comes from the Anglo Saxon, meaning 'the dairy of Willa's people'. The church has 12thC origins but had major restoration in the 19thC. It is well worth a visit and the building next to it – Upper Court – is an interesting 16thC house.* Follow the road around the churchyard to where the buildings end, then after a further 5 yards go over a stile on your RIGHT into a field with an orchard on your RIGHT. At the end of the orchard cross over a stile on your RIGHT and then through a gate into a meadow. Follow the fence on your LEFT to a stile onto a minor road.

Once there look down into the wood for a gap in the trees half way along the edge of the wood. Follow this gap to the far side of the wood, then turn LEFT along the edge of the wood – where there is no clear path – to a stile in the RIGHT corner into a meadow. Cross it diagonally to a stile, half way along the fence opposite, into the next meadow. Then continue diagonally uphill across this large meadow to a gate in the top RIGHT corner onto a minor road. Turn RIGHT and follow the road to its junction with the A465. Turn LEFT to go downhill to Stoke Lacy village and the start.

BACKBURY HILL & PENTALOE GLEN

DESCRIPTION A 5 mile walk, which can shortened to 3½ miles. The area is a haven for wildlife. If you are quiet you are almost certain to see fallow deer. The walk is over rolling country through woods and farmland and involves a gradual ascent of 500 ft and one short, steep, downhill section. There is a pub – the Moon Inn – in Mordiford about 1 mile into the walk.

START From Swardon Quarry car park and picnic site 5 miles south east of Hereford. Grid reference SO 578386.

DIRECTIONS Take A438 signed for LEDBURY. On the outskirts of the city centre and 100 yards passed the Fire Station turn RIGHT signed 'FOWNHOPE B4224'. After 3½ miles cross the bridge over the River Lugg at MORDIFORD and turn LEFT signed 'DORMINGTON'. After nearly 1 mile turn RIGHT signed for a picnic site and CHECKLEY. After 200 yards turn LEFT, then keep RIGHT and uphill for a further ½ mile to SWARDON QUARRY picnic site and car park on your RIGHT.

I *Before you start go up the slope at the LEFT of the Quarry to the viewing point for a magnificent panorama of over much of Herefordshire.* Start the walk with your back to the quarry and go up the road for 10 yards to a track off to the RIGHT. Then after a few more yards turn LEFT into a belt of woodland and go uphill through it for 140 yards to a sign for the Mordiford Loop Walk. Turn RIGHT here over a stile onto a wide grassy path. Continue along this path for ⅓ mile, crossing a track, until you reach a gate and stile into a meadow. Keep to the fence on your RIGHT initially, then go through a wide gateway gap, and now go downhill with the fence on your LEFT. At the bottom of the field enter a wood and follow the path downhill, ignoring a cross track after 15 yards. Towards the end of the wood there is a short steep section and finally some steps down

onto a metalled track. Turn RIGHT and go downhill to the main road.

2 If you require refreshment then turn RIGHT here for the Moon Inn 100 yds along the road. To continue the walk turn LEFT and after 150 yards turn LEFT at a Mordiford Loop Walk finger post and follow a narrow path to join a residential road. After the third bungalow on the LEFT, turn LEFT down a narrow fenced path to a gate into a meadow. Then follow Pentaloe Brook on your LEFT through two meadows. *This brook is the setting for Mordiford folklore. A dragon, which came here to drink had become a nuisance and it was decided to eliminate it. A prisoner volunteered for the task in return for his freedom. He hid in a barrel and shot the dragon with an arrow aimed through the bung hole. Sadly the dying fiery breath of the dragon set the barrel alight and its occupant!* At the end of the second meadow, with a derelict cottage ahead, do not cross the brook but turn RIGHT along the cottage boundary fence to a stile into Bear's Wood. After 40 yards into the wood keep LEFT on joining a wider track until you emerge onto an open area at the end of a main forest track. *The Mordiford Loop walk goes straight ahead here on a very muddy footpath (if you want to take this route it is shown on the map).* Turn RIGHT to go uphill on the main forest road. *As you ascend look on the RIGHT among the conifers for ant hills, some several feet high, made by wood ants.* After ½ mile, where the road turns sharp RIGHT back on itself, in the far LEFT corner of the bend, a narrow path leads downhill to the LEFT to a stile into a meadow. Aim for lowest corner of the wood ahead. Go into Limburies Wood and follow the footpath, keeping to the edge of the wood, until it emerges onto a main track. Turn LEFT, cross the brook to a stile 30 yards ahead on the RIGHT. The short walk leaves the main walk here.

3 Turn RIGHT over the stile and follow the brook through three fields. At the end of the third cross the stile and turn RIGHT over a footbridge into an old orchard. Go ahead keeping parallel to the hedge on the LEFT to another footbridge into an orchard. Now

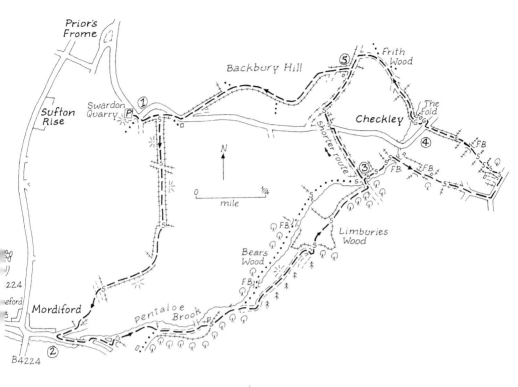

follow.the hedge on the RIGHT to keep to the RIGHT of a fenced remains of a building. Then follow the fence on the LEFT to a gate and stile into a green lane. Continue to a metalled road, ignore roads to LEFT and RIGHT, go straight ahead. At the next road junction turn LEFT. Then after Woodside Cottage on your LEFT turn LEFT into an orchard and continue straight ahead through three fields to a stile onto a footpath between fences and after passing a house on the LEFT join a minor road.

4 Turn RIGHT here for 30 yards and then LEFT into the entrance to The Fold. Go through the gate on the LEFT and follow the track over the brook. Follow a footpath between hedges into a wood. Once in the wood ignore all paths and tracks to both RIGHT and LEFT and keep on the main track going gently uphill until you emerge from the wood onto another track. Turn LEFT and then go a few yards to turn RIGHT where the

track forks before a white cottage. The short walk rejoins here.

5 Go uphill on the track, after 150 yards turn RIGHT off the track onto a footpath signed 'Loop Walk' to continue uphill with a fence on the LEFT. Stay on this main path for over ¹/₂ mile until you reach a minor road. Turn RIGHT for 50 yards then turn LEFT off the road onto a grassy path into a belt of trees and follow this path back to the quarry.

THE 3 ¹/₂ MILE WALK

Follow the main route to point **3**, then continue up the track to join a minor road. Turn LEFT for 25 yards to go over a stile on your RIGHT into a meadow. Follow the fence on your RIGHT uphill to a stile to turn RIGHT onto a track. Follow the track to a white cottage on the LEFT just before the track forks. Turn LEFT at this track junction. You have now rejoined the main walk at point **5**.

BROCKHAMPTON & THE RIVER WYE

DESCRIPTION A 3³/₄ mile walk over varied terrain of woodland, farmland and along a lovely stretch of the River Wye. The full walk involves one short steep down and another steep uphill section but these can be avoided on the short walk of 2¹/₂ miles. The walk starts at the beautifully unique 20thC church of All Saints Brockhampton. The opportunity for a visit, either before or after the walk, should not be missed. If the River Wye is in flood, follow the shorter walk.

START Brockhampton church 8 miles South East of Hereford. Grid reference SO 594321.

DIRECTIONS Take A465 towards LEDBURY. On the outskirts of the city centre and 200 yards passed the Fire Station turn RIGHT signed 'FOWNHOPE B4224'. Follow for 7 miles to FOWNHOPE. Turn RIGHT at the cross roads immediately before the church signed 'CAPLER and BROCKHAMPTON CHURCH'. Follow for 1¹/₂ miles to turn LEFT at the cross roads and go downhill for 300 yards to park on the road by the church.

I *Brockhampton church was built in 1902 and described by the architectural authority, Nicholaus Pevsner, as 'One of the most convincing and most impressive of churches of its date in any country'. The architect and builder was Lethaby, a desciple of William Morris and the Arts & Crafts movement. Indeed there are two tapestries one each side of the altar made in the William Morris Workshop from designs by Edward Burne-Jones. The church is lovingly maintained by its parishioners even to the hand embroidered prayer book covers, each with a different wild flower. It is a must for a visit.* Now with your back to the Lych Gate cross the road and turn RIGHT for 20 yards to a gate into a meadow and go down the valley. *As you descend Brockhampton Court will become visible on your LEFT. Rebuilt in 1893 from an 18c rectory it was the home of Alice Foster, and her husband*

of the Yorkshire milling family, who had the church built in memory of her parents. It is now a Residential Home. At the end of the meadow go over a stile to turn RIGHT onto a minor road. Follow uphill to a road junction. Cross the junction to a track leading uphill between hedges to enter a field. Now follow the track with a hedge on your RIGHT through two fields. At the end of the second field go through the gate and then turn immediately RIGHT over a stile and follow the hedge on your RIGHT to join a grassy green lane. Turn LEFT and follow it until it ends at an arable field. Turn RIGHT here and follow the track with the hedge on your LEFT until you reach a minor road. The short walk leaves the main walk here.

2 Turn LEFT along the road for 700 yards to a signed Picnic Site on your RIGHT. Take the track in the RIGHT corner of the site going downhill through the trees – mainly Sweet Chestnut. If it is wet be careful, especially on a short steep section, as the track is metalled and the stones can be slippery. On reaching the River Wye turn RIGHT along the bank. *First pause though to take in the beautiful view ahead of the wooded escarpment coming down to the river. The woods at the highest point hide the Iron Age Hill Fort of Capler Camp occupied between 500BC and 200/300AD.* Continue along the river bank until a track bears away from the river going gently uphill into Capler Wood and follow it to a minor road. Turn RIGHT and go uphill for 700 yards, involving a short steep section of 1 in 6, to a Viewing Point on your RIGHT.

3 Pause here for the spectacular view down the Wye Valley. Now with your back to the Viewing Point cross the road and turn RIGHT for a few yards to turn LEFT onto a very short length of track. After 20 yards it becomes a footpath with a hedge on your RIGHT. *There are now completely different views with Capler Camp above you, then Marcle Ridge and Mast (**Walk 3**) to the East, May Hill with its distinctive crown of trees to the South East and the Forest of Dean along the skyline from south to south west.* Continue through two fields and over two stiles. A few yards after the second, turn

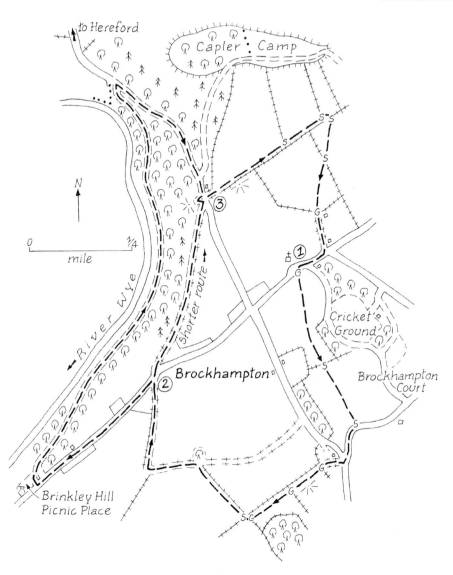

RIGHT over another stile into a meadow. Cross this diagonally to a stile in the hedge on your RIGHT. Continue diagonally across the next arable field to a gate on the RIGHT of a house. Go through the gate and down a short lane to a minor road. Turn RIGHT and go 150 yards downhill back to the start.

THE 2½ MILE WALK

Follow the main walk to point **2**, then cross over the minor road and after a few yards turn LEFT onto a waymarked Wye Valley Walk track. Follow this for nearly ½ mile passing houses and gardens on your RIGHT and with woods on your LEFT to join a minor road. Turn LEFT for a few yards to the Viewing Point. You have now rejoined the main walk at point **3**.

SHUCKNALL & WESTHIDE

DESCRIPTION A 3 mile walk over Shucknall Hill and through woods and farmland and the peaceful unspoilt village of Westhide. The route is on good firm and well defined tracks and paths. It involves a total ascent of about 450 ft but the climbs are gentle over both Shucknall Hill and White Hill. There are though two steep short downhill sections but apart from these it would be graded as an 'Easy' walk. Even though the route is mainly wooded there are many opportunities for panoramic views over the surrounding countryside.

START Off the road at Shucknall 5½ miles east of Hereford. Grid reference SO 587427.

DIRECTIONS Take A4103 towards WORCESTER. After 5½ miles at the SHUCKNALL boundary road sign continue for a further ½ mile to turn LEFT onto a minor road signed 'SHUCKNALL HILL' and opposite a bus stop on the RIGHT. Go up the hill and take the first turning RIGHT and after 30 yards park on the LEFT.

I Continue up the road for 80 yards. Take the first track on your LEFT after the driveway to Hill Croft. Go uphill on this track between fenced properties. On reaching a cross track go straight ahead with an open village green on your RIGHT. Continue on this track passing to the LEFT of a house ahead to where the track ends at a reservoir on the LEFT. Go ahead to enter Westhide Wood. A good path now leads you through this attractive mixed broadleaved wood with predominantly oak, beech and sweet chestnut. *In Spring it is a mass of bluebells.* Level at first there is then a brief steepish downhill section only to climb back up again but this time more gently. *It explains the Camel's Back name for this part of the wood.* Continue in a more or less straight line through the wood ignoring all tracks to RIGHT or LEFT until you reach a stile into a meadow.

2 Cross the meadow keeping parallel to the hedge on the RIGHT to a gate into a green lane. *A little way into the meadow pause for the view. To your LEFT (or West) Withington church spire appears over the trees, then to the North West the silhouettes of two triangular hills, 10 miles away, rising dramatically out of the plain between wooded ridges. The larger is Pyon Hill – a conical wooded hill and although only 590 ft high is a landmark recognised for many miles around.* Follow the lane until it joins a minor road. As you near the road the well manicured gardens of Westhide Court come into view on the RIGHT. Turn RIGHT onto the road to pass The Lodge and Porch House on the RIGHT. *A short diversion may be of interest here to see the old hop kilns of the Westhide Estate – if so turn RIGHT at the Westhide Estate sign into the walled road to the hop kilns 150 yards ahead on the LEFT. As you approach them you will pass the entrance to the imposing Georgian Westhide Court.* Now retrace your steps back to the Estate sign and turn RIGHT. St. Bartholomew's Church is now ahead on the RIGHT. It has a pyramidal roofed 12c tower but the main body of the church was rebuilt in 1867. In spring the churchyard is covered in snowdrops. Follow the road around until it turns LEFT. Turn RIGHT here through a gate onto a track which after passing through another gate becomes a footpath with a small lake on the RIGHT. Continue to join a surfaced lane.

3 Turn LEFT and go gently uphill with derelict kennels on the RIGHT. Where the lane turns sharp LEFT ignore two tracks ahead and keep on the lane. Shortly after the trees end on the LEFT the lane becomes a track. Now follow this track for nearly ½ mile with the woods on the RIGHT. *There are fine views along this section towards Stoke Hill (**Walk 8**).* Shortly after the track enters woods on both sides, it turns sharp RIGHT, ignore a grassy track ahead going downhill and stay on the main track going gently uphill until it passes a bungalow on the RIGHT. From now on it becomes a grassy track between a new plantation. At the top of the hill there is a small reservoir

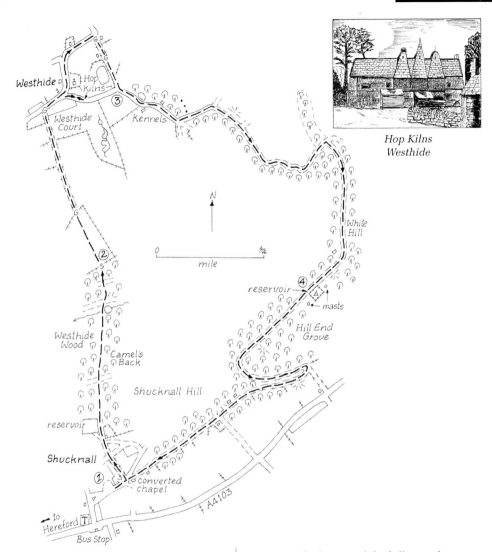

Hop Kilns
Westhide

and a tri-angulation point between two tele-phone masts. *From this area there are views across the the Wye and Lugg valleys between Backbury Hill (Walk 9) and the tree cladded Aconbury Iron Age Hill Fort at 900 feet, 5 miles to the south of Hereford.*

4 Continue on the grassy track, now going gontly downhill, until it seems to end at denser and more mature woodland. You will discover that there is a track on the LEFT going quite steeply downhill through the trees. Near the bottom of the hill turn sharp RIGHT at a track junction, almost doubling back on yourself, along a more level track. *Below you there is a garden seat to enjoy the superb views of the full 8 mile range of the Malvern Hills 10 miles away to the east. Alas the seat is on the wrong side of the fence and for the benefit of the land owner only!* Follow the track for ¹/₂ mile until it joins a surfaced lane at a converted chapel on the LEFT. Go down the lane 100 yards to return to the start.

WALK 12
WEOBLEY

DESCRIPTION An easy 5 mile walk around one of the most attractive and best kept villages in the UK. Weobley, the jewel of Herefordshire, is probably the best known of all the Black and White villages. The walk is over open farm and parkland on well used paths and tracks. There are hotels, restaurants, pubs and coffee shops in the village and a pub half-way around. See the map for an optional short cut to make a 3 mile walk.

START In Bell Square, Weobley, 10 miles north west of Hereford. Grid reference SO 402517.

DIRECTIONS Take A438 towards BRECON. After 2½ miles turn RIGHT immediately after the WYEVALE GARDEN CENTRE onto A480 and follow this for 7 miles to turn RIGHT onto B4230 signed 'WEOBLEY 3'. In WEOBLEY go straight ahead at the first junction then turn RIGHT at the next and park on the LEFT in Bell Square adjacent to the Telephone Exchange.

I Walk uphill turning RIGHT at the Red Lion into the centre of the village. As you go up the main street keep RIGHT at the bus shelter. *The village rose garden, now below you, was once the market place with half-timbered buildings but was destroyed by fire in 1943. Magnus, the magpie, is now perched there – a symbol of the Black and White village. This striking sculpture celebrates winning The Village of the Year award in 1999 and the Millennium. The name Weobley derives from Weobba, a 6thC Mercian prince who established an outpost here.* At the T junction at the top of the road cross the road and take the track opposite between two cottages to a gate into the grounds of the site of a 12thC castle. Follow the path through the ramparts to a gate into a meadow. Cross the meadow to the far RIGHT corner. Go through the gate, and with a hedge on the RIGHT, continue to the end of the field.

2 Turn LEFT here for a few yards then through a gate on the RIGHT into a meadow with a fence on your LEFT.

Continue until you reach the wood ahead then turn RIGHT along its edge to a gate onto a lane. Shortly after passing a house on your LEFT, turn LEFT through a gate into a field. Go diagonally across it to a gate in the far top LEFT corner to join a track. *There are now parkland views to the LEFT where Garnstone Castle once stood, built by Nash in 1805 but demolished in 1959.* Follow the track until it passes through a belt of woodland onto a road. Turn LEFT down the road for 30 yards then RIGHT along a minor road signed to Marshpools Inn. Follow this road to the first junction and turn RIGHT. After 50 yards turn LEFT through a gate and then follow the hedge on the RIGHT to the end of the field. Turn LEFT onto a road and after 100 yards turn RIGHT onto a road signed Private Road. Go to where the road, which becomes a track, ends at Stone House. Now turn RIGHT along a fenced footpath between Stone House and Rose Tree Cottage to a stile into a field. Turn LEFT for 30 yards to go over a stile into a field on the LEFT. Follow the hedge on your RIGHT to climb over some low hurdles into a meadow. Cross it diagonally to a stile, to the LEFT of a house, onto a road. Cross the road and over another stile, then go diagonally across the field to another stile.

3 Go over the stile and cross the next two fields diagonally to a stile at the corner of a hedge on the far side of the second field. Now with the hedge on your LEFT continue along two more fields, ignoring two gates on your LEFT, to a gate into a short length of green lane leading to a minor road. Cross over the road to a stile a few yards to your LEFT and then cross the next field diagonally to a stile into a meadow. Continue diagonally to a gap in the hedge ahead and then make for the far RIGHT corner of the field, with houses beyond, to a stile into a green lane. Follow this lane, ignoring footpaths off to the LEFT, until it becomes an asphalt path and joins a road.

4 Cross the road, turn LEFT along the pavement for 40 yards then turn RIGHT between houses. Follow this footpath through a residential area keeping LEFT until the path emerges to go between the fenced

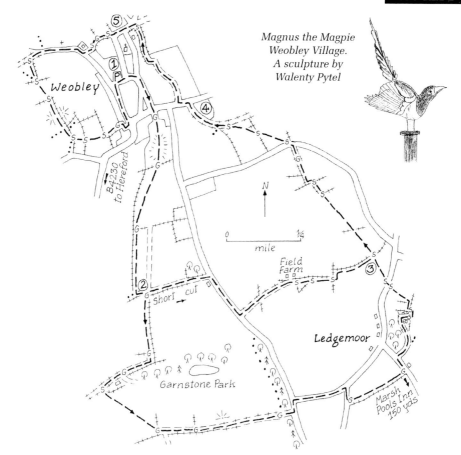

*Magnus the Magpie
Weobley Village.
A sculpture by
Walenty Pytel*

edge of a field and a handrail above a ditch. Continue to where it ends at a gate onto a track. Turn LEFT for a few yards to an intersection of tracks and gates. Just keep LEFT at this complex junction and go towards the church. *The church of St Peter and St Paul dates from 13thC and has a magnificent spire – the second highest in Herefordshire – hence the saying 'Poor Weobley, proud people, low Church and high steeple'.* Ignore the first turning on the LEFT, continue along the churchyard wall to where the road turns LEFT.

5 Turn RIGHT here off the road over a stile into a paddock. Keep to the hedge on your LEFT, then through gates to a stile onto a path between gardens to the main road. Turn RIGHT along the pavement pass-

ing a half-timbered red house and the Roman Catholic church. Then after another 100 yards cross over the road to go up a track for 50 yards to cross a stile on your LEFT. Go up the hill with a hedge on your LEFT to a stile into a field. Cross the field to a stile opposite and, now with the hedge on your LEFT, climb to the top of the hill *where there is a seat to enjoy the 360 degree panorama.* Now continue downhill, ignoring the first stile on the LEFT to cross the next one, where there is a change of direction in the hedge, into a meadow. Now cross three fields in the general direction of the village centre until a gate leads you into a yard. Keep RIGHT to another gate onto the road. Turn LEFT along the road for 200 yards, then turn RIGHT back to the start.

SUTTON WALLS

DESCRIPTION An easy 3 mile walk, which can be shortened to 2½ miles, around the ancient Iron Age Hill Fort of Sutton Walls. The route rises from 200 feet at its lowest point at the start to 300 feet on the top of Sutton Walls Fort. Both ascent and descent are gradual. The Fort, as you would expect from a strategic and fortified settlement, provides some fine panoramas of the surrounding countryside.

START In Marden village on the road by the telephone box and the butcher's shop. Grid reference SO 522475.

DIRECTIONS Take the A49 towards LEOMINSTER. After 3½ miles turn RIGHT signed 'MARDEN 2'. Go through the village of MORETON ON LUGG. At the first junction after the level crossing keep LEFT and continue for ½ mile, keeping RIGHT, into the village. Park on the road by the first shops and telephone box on the LEFT.

1 Face the farm building opposite you, and turn RIGHT for 70 yards then cross the road to a footpath finger post sign. Cross over the stile onto a track between bungalows to a gate into a field. Follow the hedgerow, initially on your RIGHT, but changing to the LEFT and then back again to the RIGHT, over three stiles in a more or less straight line and going gently uphill until you reach a stile into the wooded slopes of the fort. *Before crossing this stile look back to take in the fine views. Starting from your RIGHT there is the long wooded ridge of Queens Wood to Westhope Hill, then two wooded triangular hills rise dramatically from the plain. These distinctive landmarks are Pyon Hill and Butthouse Knapp, or known locally as Robin Hoods Butts, and then finally on the LEFT is the wooded Badnage Hill.* Cross over the stile and go into the wood for 10 yards to where the path divides.

2 *The fort covers 30 acres and was occupied until about 300 AD when it was attacked by the Romans and abandoned. A large number of skeletons with warlike injuries were found during archeological survey and excavation in 1948 which supports the view that the Romans slaughtered the fort's inhabitants. Subsequently the fort was used for gravel extraction and when that was abandoned, controversially and much against a strong conservation lobby, the hole was filled with highly toxic waste from the Midlands. As predicted, leaching occured and there were parts of the hillside where nothing would grow. The site has since been properly sealed and capped.* To take advantage of the views from the fort, the walk now takes a meandering route around it. If you want to shorten the walk by ½ mile then turn LEFT here and rejoin the guide at point **3**. For the full walk turn RIGHT and follow the level footpath around the western end of the fort. *Pause for the view from a gap in the hedgerow at the South West corner of the fort. The top of the Black Mountain range is on the RIGHT and there is a glimpse of the Malvern Hills on the LEFT.* Continue on this path until you drop down to a track entering the fort. Turn LEFT here and go up the track to the level plateau at the top of the fort. To continue ignore an intersection of tracks and go straight ahead downhill, initially on a narrow footpath between bushes. You are now back where you first entered the fort. Turn RIGHT.

3 Follow the wide path through the trees at the base of the ramparts until you come to overhead power lines at the end of the fort. Turn LEFT here through a 35 yard belt of trees to join a footpath at the edge of the wood. *Again pause to take in the panorama. To your RIGHT is Backbury Hill* (**Walk 9**), *then the Malvern Hills straight ahead and Titterstone in the Clee Hills some 20 miles away to the LEFT.* Turn LEFT and go downhill with the hedge on your LEFT to a stile in the corner of the field into an orchard. Take a few steps to the LEFT then continue downhill with a windbreak hedge on your RIGHT to join a track through the orchard. *The trees in this part of the orchard are all dessert apples and are pruned so that they can be picked by hand without the use of ladders.* Follow the track when it turns RIGHT toward some buildings and a

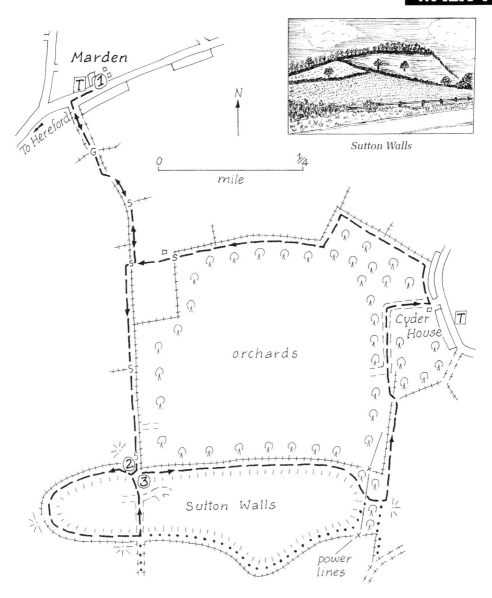

Sutton Walls

minor road. Before you reach the road turn LEFT opposite Cyder House and follow the fence on your RIGHT, at first alongside some gardens and then it becomes the hedge to a field. Follow this hedge, with two changes in direction, for ½ mile to a stile at the end of the orchard. *They are all cider apple trees in* *this part of the orchard.* Cross the stile into an arable field, keeping an old shed to your RIGHT, to a stile straight ahead. Do not cross the stile but turn RIGHT to rejoin the footpath you started out on. Retrace you steps back to the start.

BREINTON SPRINGS & WYEVALE WOOD

DESCRIPTION An easy 5½ mile walk which because of its figure of eight configuration can be walked as two separate circular walks of 1½ or 4 miles. Additionally the map shows a short cut on the 4 mile loop, reducing it to 3½ miles. The full walk covers a variety of terrain including a beautiful stretch along the River Wye, over farmland, through woods and a nature reserve. The walk involves ascents and descents of 245 feet but all the hills are gentle slopes.

START From the National Trust Car Park (there is no charge) at Breinton Springs 2½ miles west of Hereford. Grid reference SO 472396.

DIRECTIONS Take the A49 towards ROSS ON WYE and get into RIGHT hand lane as soon as possible. After 300 yards filter RIGHT at the traffic lights (immediately before the bridge over the River Wye) and turn RIGHT into BARTON ROAD. Continue into BREINTON ROAD keeping LEFT at its junction with WESTFALING STREET. After BROOMY HILL WATERWORKS keep LEFT signed for 'BREINTON CHURCH'. Continue for 1 mile to BREINTON CHURCH signed turning, then after a further 200 yards turn LEFT into the lane for the car park

I Leave the car park by the pedestrian gate and turn LEFT towards Breinton Church. Keep the church on your LEFT and go through a gate onto a footpath at the top of a wooded bank. Follow this path with an orchard on the LEFT to a stile into a field. Now with a hedge on your RIGHT continue to a stile half way along the field. Cross into a meadow and now with the hedge on your LEFT follow it until you come to a stile into the garden of Warham House. Do not cross this stile but turn RIGHT here to go downhill through a gap in an intermittent hedgerow to a stile in the LEFT corner of the field onto the riverside path. Turn RIGHT and follow the riverbank along two fields and then

across a third to a gate onto a track going uphill through the trees. Before you ascend the track go ahead through a gap in the bushes to Breinton Spring itself, where the water comes straight out of the rock at the bottom of the bank. Retrace your steps to ascend the path from the gate back to the car park.

2 From the car park go along the road and just after the entrance to a house with ornamental gate posts cross a stile on the LEFT to bypass a tennis court on the RIGHT. Follow the path diagonally through the next little paddock to a gate in the corner onto a minor road. Cross the road and go up a short track with a house on the RIGHT to cross a stile on the LEFT into a field. Now keep LEFT along the hedgerow to a stile into the next meadow. Again follow the hedge on the LEFT to a stile and footbridge onto a minor road. Turn RIGHT here and at the first junction turn LEFT, then continue until you reach a track on your LEFT.

3 Turn LEFT here, with the farm buildings of Manor House Farm on the RIGHT, up this fenced/hedged track and follow it uphill until you reach a gate into a meadow. Keep straight ahead across this meadow to the RIGHT hand of two gates. *Enjoy the panorama at this the highest point of your walk at 360 feet.* Go through the gate and follow the hedge on your LEFT to a stile in the corner of the field onto a track. Cross this stile and immediately turn RIGHT across another stile into the wood. A path now keeps to the top of the wood to a stile into a meadow. Continue through two fields and an orchard keeping to the hedge on your RIGHT. At the bottom of the hill in the orchard turn RIGHT over a stile onto a short path through the trees to another stile into a field. Turn LEFT and follow the field boundary until you reach a minor road at a T-junction. Cross the road and continue straight ahead along this cul-de-sac lane with houses on the LEFT. Where it ends, at the entrance to a Caravan Park, continue ahead along a fenced path

until it reaches an intersection of tracks and a wood on the LEFT.

4 Turn LEFT here for 20 yards and then RIGHT into Wyevale Wood. *This is a Herefordshire Nature Trust Reserve donated by Mr Williamson, the founder of Wyevale Garden Centres. There is a bird hide near the entrance which visitors are welcome to use. Look for nuthatch and spotted woodpecker.* There are several routes through the Reserve but the one shown on the sketch map follows the LEFT hand boundary – but whatever route you use aim to end up in the far RIGHT corner of the Reserve to go through a gate onto a green lane. *This was once a drovers route from Wales to Hereford.* Turn LEFT onto the lane and follow until you reach a pond on your RIGHT. Turn RIGHT after it along a track passing Upper Hill Farm on your LEFT. When you reach the road turn

RIGHT and follow it to the T-junction, then keep RIGHT for a further 200 yards to a stile on the LEFT.

5 Cross the stile and follow the hedge on the LEFT along two fields to a gate in the corner of the second onto a short length of lane to join a road. You are now back in Lower Breinton. Turn LEFT onto the road and then RIGHT at the next junction back to the car park.

THE 4 MILE WALK
Start at point **2** on the main walk and follow it to the end.

THE 1½ MILE WALK
Follow the main walk to point **2**.

PENGETHLEY, RIVER WYE & SELLACK

DESCRIPTION A longer but easy walk of 5½ miles that can be shortened to 4½. There is refreshment available on route at the Lough Pool Inn. If the River Wye is in flood then shorter walk must be taken, but apart from this situation, the walk is on good firm tracks. The route is over varied terrain, through farmland woods and a one mile stretch along the Wye. The initial section is along a ridge with some fine panoramas. The walk involves a total ascent of 330 feet but all ascents and descents are gradual.

START From the lay-by 10 miles South of Hereford on the A49. Grid reference SO 548253.

DIRECTIONS Take the A49 towards ROSS ON WYE. After 10 miles, at the PENGETHLEY GARDEN CENTRE, continue for a further 500 yards to park in the lay-by on the LEFT.

I Walk back up the road for 350 yards to a finger post on the RIGHT signing the start of a bridleway. Turn RIGHT up this track until you reach farm buildings on the RIGHT. Continue straight ahead here, ignoring a track to the LEFT, to go through two gates (normally left open) to where the track divides. Now keep LEFT onto a green lane which soon narrows to footpath width until it emerges into an open area where several tracks converge. Turn LEFT here onto a farm track with a hedge on you RIGHT and follow it for 1 mile when it joins a minor road. *This track provides some fine views particularly after passing isolated farm buildings on the LEFT. Look half LEFT for the tall red sandstone spire of Kings Caple church 1½ miles away across the Wye valley and beyond it Backbury Hill (Walk 9). Ahead is the Marcle Ridge with its radio mast (Walk 3) and beyond are the Malvern Hills. Then half right is May Hill, the distinctive rounded hill crowned with a cluster of trees some 7 miles away. Although only 971 feet high it is*

a familiar landmark for many miles around. The shorter walk leaves the main route here.

2 Turn LEFT and go downhill on the road. At the bottom of the hill, at the junction of a minor road, turn RIGHT over a stile into a meadow. Cross the field to the river, bear RIGHT and then follow the bank along this beautiful stretch of the Wye for 1 mile to Sellack bridge. *This section of the Wye is a favourite for fishermen and you will soon pass a fishing lodge. Salmon catches of over 50 lbs have been caught in the past from this part of the river. The suspension footbridge at Sellack was built in 1895 and until then there was a ferry. Look at the memorial plinth on the bridge recording the goodwill between the two parishes either side of the river.* At the bridge turn RIGHT and make for Sellack church two fields away.

3 *The church has 12thC origins. There is a most unusual gravestone in the churchyard near the east end of the north aisle – it simply reads 'GONE' with a finger pointing to the heavens!* Leaving the church turn LEFT along the road to just before the first cottage on the RIGHT. Turn RIGHT here over a stile into a meadow. Now go gently uphill keeping parallel to the hedge on the RIGHT to a stile into a wood. The path now divides, ignore a track going uphill, take the level one and after a few more yards, again ignore a track going downhill to the stream. Go through the wood, on what soon becomes a narrow path, to a stile into a meadow. Go straight ahead keeping to the lowest part of the valley to a stile to the LEFT of a house at the far side of the meadow. Cross the stile onto a fenced path to another stile onto a minor road. Cross the road and on your LEFT is the Lough Pool Inn.

4 Go up the minor road with the Inn on your LEFT. Continue for nearly ½ mile keeping RIGHT at the first road junction then at the second, immediately after a large ornamental pond, turn RIGHT onto a track signed for the Grove Cattery. Continue to where the track divides and turn RIGHT and go to the end of a short track, with a house on the RIGHT, to cross a stile on the LEFT

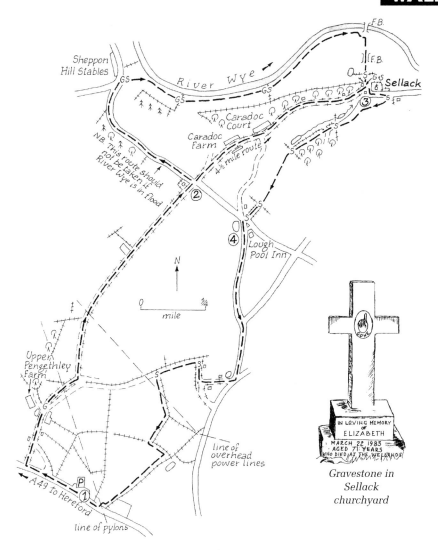

*Gravestone in
Sellack
churchyard*

into a field. Go uphill with a hedge on the RIGHT to a stile ahead into the next field. Cross the stile and turn LEFT. Now follow the hedgerow to the second corner in the field to go through a gap in the hedge there and turn LEFT into the next field. Now follow the hedge downhill into the corner of that field and then turn sharp RIGHT to follow the field boundary uphill until it reaches the A49 road under the pyloned power lines. Turn RIGHT and walk 50 yards up the road back to the start point.

THE 4½ MILE WALK

Follow the main walk to point **2**, then go straight ahead across the road and follow a wide track passing through Caradoc farm and stables and then passing Caradoc Court. *The latter has its origins as an Elizabethan Manor House rebuilt in its present style in 1864. It was seriously damaged by fire in 1986 and is currently being restored.* Continue downhill on the track until you reach the church. You have now rejoined the main walk at point **3**.

About the author, Mike Thompson . . .

Mike Thompson's childhood was spent in London. His first introduction to the countryside was in 1953, during his apprenticeship, when he was sent to the Outward Bound School in Mid Wales – to toughen him up! Instead the result was a love affair with Wales and the Marches which continues to this day.
On his retirement in 1989 he moved to the area and took up guiding walks. A few years later he wrote the first guide in this series – *Local Walks Around Machynlleth* – which has been revised and is still in print. He now lives in Herefordshire within sight of his beloved Welsh mountains and is still enthusiastically walking. His regular Sunday afternoon guided walks for local church congregations are the basis of the walks in this guide.

KEY TO THE MAPS

- ➤ Walk route and direction
- —— Metalled road
- – – – Unsurfaced road
- .... Footpath/route adjoining walk route
- ∿∿ River/stream
- ♣ ♧ Trees
- ▬▭▬ Railway
- G Gate
- S Stile
- ⋰ Viewpoint
- P Parking
- T Telephone

THE COUNTRY CODE

Be safe – plan ahead and follow relevant signs

Leave gates and property as you find them

Protect plants and animals, and take your litter home

Keep dogs under close control

Be considerate to other people

Published by
Kittiwake 3 Glantwymyn Village Workshops, Glantwymyn, Machynlleth, Montgomeryshire
SY20 8LY

© Text: Mike Thompson 2005
© Maps: Morag Perrott 2005
© Illustrations: Patsy Thompson 2005

Cover Pictures: Main: Queen's Wood; Inset; Hereford Cathedral. Photos by kind permission of Herefordshire Tourism © 2005

Printed by eco print, Caldicot, Gwent.

ISBN: 1 902302 34 6